PEOPLE TRAFFICKING

by Judith Anderson

A⁺

Smart Apple Media

Published by Smart Apple Media
P.O. Box 3263, Mankato, Minnesota 56002

Series editor: Jeremy Smith
Editors: Sarah Ridley and Julia Bird
Design: sprout.uk.com
Artworks: sprout.uk.com
Picture researcher: Diana Morris

Printed in the United States of America at
Corporate Graphics, in North Mankato, Minnesota.

Published by arrangement with the Watts Publishing
Group LTD, London.

Library of Congress Cataloging-in-Publication Data

Anderson, Judith, 1965-
People trafficking / Judith Anderson.
p. cm.—(Inside crime)
Includes index.
Summary: "Delves into the worldwide problem
of people trafficking, describing the issue and
the practices various organizations use to catch
traffickers. Includes real-life examples and in-
depth case studies from around the world"—
Provided by publisher.
ISBN 978-1-59920-397-3 (library binding)
1. Human trafficking—Juvenile literature. I. Title.
HQ281.A528 2012
364.15—dc22
                                    2010042512

Picture credits: AFP/Getty Images: 27. Sunday
Alamba/AP/PAI: 30. Mary Altaffer/AP/PAI: 39. Luis
M. Alvarez /PAI: 41. Eliaria Andrade/Globo/Getty
Images: 25. Antislavery International/Panos: 10.
AP/PAI: 11, 12. Mark Baker/AP /PAI: 32. Ruls Brekke/
AFP/Getty Images: 31b. © Kay Cernush for the
U.S. State Department: 14, 17, 21t, 36, 37t, 37b.
Denis Charlet/AFP/Getty Images: 33. Paul Cooper/
Rex Features: front cover br. Baz Czerwinski/AP/
PAI: 29bl. Rachid Dahnoun/Alamy: front cover bl.
Linda Davidson/The Washington Post/Getty Images:
20. Paul Faith/PA/PAI: 19, 31t. Alexander Johns/
Alamy: front cover t, 2. Richard Jones/Rex Features:
21b. Jean-Philippe Ksiazek/AFP/Getty Images: 22.
Eduardo Martino/Panos: 8. Mike Ralston/AFP/Getty
Images: 26. Rex Features: 24. Karen Robinson/
Panos: 15, 34. Issouf Sanogo/AFP/Getty Images: 13.
STR/AFP/Getty Images: 9, 35. Andrew Testa/Panos:
23t, 38. © UNODC. All Rights Reserved.: 40bl.
Veronique de Viguerie/Getty Images: 16. Dan White/
Panos: 18. Maria Zarnayova/isifa/Getty Images: 29tr.

1411
11-2011

9 8 7 6 5 4 3 2

CONTENTS

INSIDE PICTURE

People are one of the world's most valuable resources. We provide the labor for agriculture and industry. We provide services such as cleaning, healthcare, or entertainment. It should be a fair exchange: in return for our labor or services, we are paid a wage. Yet millions of people around the world are forced by others to work for little or no wages—and they are powerless to do anything about it.

What is People Trafficking?

People trafficking means moving people away from the communities in which they live, often by force or by deception, in order to exploit them. This movement may take place across international borders, or it may be within the same country. It may even be within the same city. Common forms of exploitation include slave, bonded, or forced labor, forced marriage, forced prostitution, and using children for illegal adoption or to fight as underage soldiers.

FACT FILE

The United Nations (UN) defines people trafficking as follows:

"The recruitment, transportation, transfer, harboring, or receipt of persons, by means of the threat or use of force or other forms of coercion, of abduction, of fraud, of deception, of the abuse of power, or of a position of vulnerability or of the giving or receiving of payments or benefits to achieve the consent of a person having control over another person, for the purpose of exploitation."

A Global Epidemic

People trafficking is now the fastest-growing criminal industry in the world, and the second most profitable after the drug trade. It affects every country, crosses continents, preys on the vulnerability of its victims, and feeds off the greed of the people traffickers themselves and all those who exploit the victims' labor. Around 80 percent of all trafficking victims are women and children. While many of them are moved across borders, thousands more are trafficked within their own country, and the criminals are rarely caught.

◄ This Brazilian farm worker has spent most of his life in forced labor—forced by his employer to work for little or no pay.

TRAFFICKING IN PERSONS REPORT (2010)

The U.S. Department of State publishes an annual Trafficking in Persons Report in which it groups countries according to how it considers they are dealing with the crime within their borders.

TIER 1 Countries that fully comply with the United States' minimum standards, including Australia, the United Kingdom, Nigeria, Canada, Poland, and Croatia.

TIER 2 Countries that don't fully comply but are making significant efforts to do so, including Pakistan, Benin, Estonia, Israel, Japan, and Mexico.

TIER 2 Watch List Countries that are making efforts to comply but where numbers of victims remain high, including Chad, Bangladesh, Gabon, and Russia.

TIER 3 Countries where no significant efforts are being made, including Burma (also known as Myanmar), Zimbabwe, Iran, Saudi Arabia, and Cuba.

ON TARGET

From 2010 onward, the annual Trafficking in Persons Report will assess the United States' own response to the crime of people trafficking in the same way that it judges the responses of other countries. U.S. Secretary of State Hillary Clinton has said that this will increase the credibility of its efforts to name and shame the worst perpetrators.

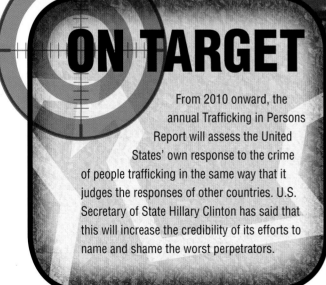

▲ *Slave children ride in the back of a police truck on the border between Nigeria and Benin. People traffickers were moving them across the border when the children were discovered and rescued in September 2003.*

HOW DID WE GET HERE?

People trafficking has always existed. However, it hasn't always been illegal. From about 1500 until the mid-19th century, people were openly captured and transported from Africa to the Americas, to endure a life of slavery. The transatlantic slave trade was abolished during the 19th century, but the exploitation of one person by another has continued in many forms around the world ever since.

Huge Profits

People trafficking is a highly lucrative business, with estimated profits of $31.6 billion a year. Victims may be moved across several borders in order to evade the police and cover the tracks of the traffickers. This costs money, so all sorts of people stand to make a profit,

ON TARGET

The United Nations favors a three-point approach in combating people trafficking:

- The prevention of people trafficking by raising awareness and tackling demand so that countries do not buy goods produced by forced labor.

- The protection for victims of people trafficking by offering temporary care and shelter.

- The prosecution and punishment of anyone involved in people trafficking.

▲ This 19th century engraving shows chained slaves at a slave auction. Two men are making a deal in the background.

from corrupt border officials to suppliers of false documents. And then there are those who profit from the forced labor itself—the gangmasters who organize their victims into labor gangs, the sex trade pimps, or the families who keep a domestic slave imprisoned in their homes.

► A border guard on the Bulgaria/Turkey border uses a high-tech sensor to search a truck for trafficked people. Some of the sensors detect heartbeats, and others detect body heat or carbon dioxide gas (exhaled by human beings).

People Smuggling

In the past few decades, many nations have introduced tough new laws to stop people entering the country illegally. But these laws have resulted in a new problem: people smuggling. People smuggling is where illegal immigrants pay someone to help them cross borders secretly—usually in order to find work. People smuggling is not the same as trafficking, because illegal immigrants have a choice and are not being forced to do anything.

Nevertheless, on arriving in their chosen country, those who have been smuggled often find that their handlers take away their passports, present them with inflated debts that they must pay back, and use threats and violence to force the new arrivals to work for them for little or no wages. In this way, the illegal immigrant frequently becomes a victim of people trafficking.

BUSTED!

In 2009, five defendants in Los Angeles, California, were found guilty of international sex trafficking for repeatedly smuggling young Guatemalan women across the border with false promises of legitimate jobs. They then used a combination of deception, rape, violence, and threats to force them into prostitution. "The defendants [used] these victims' desire for a better life to lure them into a situation where they were deprived of their basic human rights," said United States Attorney Thomas O'Brien. "No one should be victimized in this way."

THE TRAFFICKERS

People trafficking is a low risk, high reward crime. Successful prosecutions against traffickers are quite rare, partly because of the difficulty in tracking the criminals across international borders, but also because many victims are unable or reluctant to come forward. And some law enforcement agencies simply don't make this type of crime a priority.

Organized Crime

Trafficking is big business, attracting the attention of criminal gangs who may be involved in other types of crime, such as drugs or arms smuggling. Groups such as the Chinese Snakehead gangs use their international connections to reap the profits from the country of origin right through to the victim's final destination. They often use "gangmasters"—people who organize forced labor and ensure that their victims remain too intimidated or isolated to run away or report them.

▼ *Members of a child trafficking gang were brought to court in the Chinese city of Dongguan in 2005. They were accused of abducting 38 children and selling them for adoption. Ten members of the gang were sent to prison, and the leader was sentenced to death.*

FACT FILE

As of 2010, 117 countries have signed a United Nations document agreeing to prosecute people traffickers. However, it remains one of the most under-prosecuted crimes throughout the world, even in Western Europe and the United States—where many victims end up. Estimates suggest that less than 1 percent of people trafficking crime leads to a successful prosecution.

Specialized Roles

People traffickers operate on a small-scale basis, too. Often different roles are taken on by different gangs specializing in one of the following:

- Recruitment of victims

- Providing forged documents

- Transportation

▼ *People trafficking is a lucrative business. Tracking its profits is one way to catch the criminals.*

- Bribing police or border officials or airline staff

- Acting as pimps and gangmasters who control the victims

- Organizing finances and "laundering" or hiding the profits

This specialization makes it more difficult for the police to trace the traffickers.

A Hidden Problem

For a relatively small risk, traffickers can make huge profits, either from the illegal transportation and sale of their human cargo or from the cheap labor they provide. However, not all traffickers operate in gangs. The woman who brings a maid into the country from abroad then takes away her passport, locks her indoors, and terrifies her into working for no wages is a trafficker, even if she only commits a single offense. A significant proportion of traffickers are women who are known to the victims before the trafficking offense takes place.

BUSTED!

One way to identify people traffickers is to "follow the money" by tracking the profits they make. During an investigation into a child trafficking ring that operated out of Romania, police discovered a series of luxury houses in the village where the traffickers were believed to live. The average monthly income for the area was $546. The traffickers were making $13,664 each month, making them visible to the police authorities through their lavish lifestyles.

THE VICTIMS

Victims of people trafficking are usually (but not always) from less economically developed countries where employment opportunities are fewer or wages are lower. They are most commonly women, children, or young adults under the age of 24. They may be from ethnic minorities or displaced groups such as refugees. They are vulnerable people who are physically useful, desperate for work, and who may not be missed by the society they are leaving behind.

Recruitment Methods

Traffickers have to persuade or force their victims to leave their homes and travel with them. This usually involves some form of deception—promising a job, an education, a better lifestyle, or security for the victim's family. According to the United Nations Global Initiative to Fight Human Trafficking (UN.GIFT), the most common recruitment methods include:

- Recruitment via families or friends

- Purchase of children from their parents or guardians

- False marriages

- Advertisements offering work or education abroad

- Offering bar work, or work as dancers or maids

BUSTED!

In 2010, police indicted 29 people on charges of running a sex trafficking ring active in Minnesota, Ohio, and Tennessee. The men and women charged were all legal immigrants from Somalia, and forced girls as young as 13 into lives of prostitution. Some victims were runaways lured by promises of a better life if they moved in with other girls and their victimizers.

▶ *This young woman was trafficked within Thailand. She managed to escape from a sweatshop where she and other women were imprisoned and forced to work 20 hours a day in a factory making jeans. They slept on the floor of the factory and received little food and no wages.*

ON TARGET

Many countries are beginning to recognize that they cannot treat victims of trafficking as criminals or illegal immigrants. Australia has recently introduced significant changes to its laws protecting victims of people trafficking; they are no longer forced to become police informants in order to get government help and may be given a visa that allows them to stay in the country.

A Vicious Cycle

In some parts of the world, a victim's fear of going to the authorities to report what has happened to them is well-founded. Often, the best that they can hope for is that they will be deported to their home country. But without money, and often with feelings of intense shame about what has happened to them, victims become vulnerable to approaches from traffickers again.

Isolated and Frightened

Victims are often unable or unwilling to report what has happened to them because they are locked up or kept in isolation by the traffickers. They may also fear that their families will be punished, they will be prosecuted themselves for entering a country illegally, or they will be punished for working in an illegal industry such as prostitution. Some victims are too ashamed to talk about their experiences, while in some cases victims are forced to make religious vows or even forced to take part in witchcraft ceremonies to ensure that they stay silent. Other victims are simply too traumatized to speak out.

▶ *Jovita, from Lithuania, became a victim of people traffickers after she was tricked into traveling to Germany to take a job in a hotel. When she arrived at the hotel, she was forced into prostitution and resold several times before she managed to escape.*

FORCED LABOR

No one really knows how many people around the world are forced to work in appalling conditions for little or no pay. So much of this type of crime goes undetected, and its victims often see no advantage in coming forward. But the International Labor Organization estimates that there are at least 12.3 million people in forced labor worldwide. Of this, some 2.4 million are in forced labor as a result of trafficking.

Understanding the Problem

Forced labor most frequently occurs in countries where there is less official regulation of industries such as agriculture, fishing, domestic work, quarrying, mining, and factory work. Sometimes whole communities are forced through poverty to work for excessively low wages, but those who are trafficked tend to be held against their will; they may be locked up, have their passports taken away, or put to work on a ship or in a remote location where there is little chance of escape.

▼ *A young worker sorts stones in a gravel pit in Burkina Faso. Remote locations can make it easier for employers to exploit their workers.*

BUSTED!

In 2009, two traffickers were arrested in Thailand for smuggling in 18 Burmese men and forcing them to work as fishermen in order to pay back "costs." The fishermen had been padlocked into a single room every night to prevent them from escaping. After a tip-off, the police raided two boats and freed the men.

▲ This nine-year-old Indian girl works seven days a week in a brick factory. Her whole family was trafficked within India and sold to the owner of the factory as bonded laborers.

ON TARGET

In 2004, 21 Chinese cockle pickers drowned while working in Morecambe Bay in the United Kingdom. They had been smuggled into the country illegally with the promise of well-paid work, but in fact they were paid very little and their lives were tightly controlled by a foreman. This foreman was later convicted of their manslaughter for failing to ensure adequate safeguards. In an effort to prevent similar abuses, the government set up an agency to oversee industries. All foreman are now required to register with the agency, with penalties of up to 10 years in prison for those who fail to do so.

Debt Bondage

Debt bondage is where a person's labor is demanded as a means of repayment for a loan. Many victims of trafficking may be forced to hand over their wages to repay a hugely inflated "loan" to those who have smuggled them into the country. The victims may originally have agreed to settle such a debt, but when they arrive at their destination their wages are so low, or the amounts deducted for food and shelter are so high, that they are never able to repay the money. Nor are they allowed to work for anyone else. The children of bonded laborers grow up bound to do the same jobs as their parents and have little chance of release.

A False Promise

Forced labor also occurs in the wealthier countries of the developed world. In 2007, 11 Filipinos traveled to Canada with official permits and promises of well-paid work. However, when they arrived, their new boss took away their passports and permits and drove them to a run-down bungalow where they had to sleep four to a bed and work excessive hours doing menial jobs for very little pay. When they complained, their boss threatened them with deportation. The men were finally rescued by officials from the Philippine Embassy. They have since found new jobs with fair pay and conditions.

THE SEX INDUSTRY

Of all the reported trafficking cases worldwide, 80 percent involve sexual exploitation. The victims are mainly women and children. Some are abducted, while others are enticed abroad by promises of work as waitresses or dancers, only to find themselves living in brothels and forced by their handlers to work as prostitutes for up to 16 hours a day.

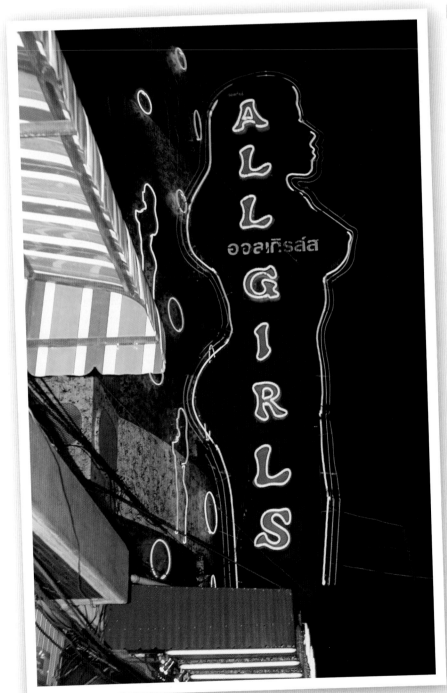

◀ Some people traffickers sell their victims to brothels, where the girls and young women are "sold" over and over again to customers who pay for sex.

Decriminalizing the Victims

In some countries, prostitution in any form is illegal, and women forced into sex work may be treated as criminals themselves. Agencies such as the United Nations are working hard to convince governments to change their laws so that anyone who is forced into the sex industry is helped and supported, rather than punished. Significantly, the UN considers all child sex workers to be victims of trafficking, even if they have not been forced into it.

Sex Trafficking and Drugs

However, the police still find it difficult to identify those who are being forced to work as prostitutes. This is often because traffickers control their victims in subtle ways. They may seek out a vulnerable girl and offer "love" and protection, while encouraging her to become addicted to drugs such as heroin. The pimp then tells the girl she must work as a prostitute in order to pay off her drug "debt." Prostitution and drugs form a vicious cycle: the more drugs she uses, the more money she owes her pimp.

BUSTED!

In June 2009, a court in Ghana sentenced three Chinese traffickers, James Xu Jin, Chou Xiou Ving, and Sam Shan Zifan, to a total of 41 years in prison. The traffickers had lured Chinese women to Ghana with promises of work in a restaurant there. However, when the women arrived, they discovered that no such restaurant existed. The traffickers confiscated their passports and forced them to work as prostitutes, keeping the profits for themselves.

◄ *This woman is being led away by police after a raid on a house in Belfast, Northern Ireland. The police rescued a number of women who had been forced into prostitution after being trafficked from China.*

Sex Trafficking Crackdown

In a 2009 crackdown on child sex trafficking called Operation Cross Country, U.S. federal officials arrested nearly 700 people and rescued 52 children in 36 cities across the nation. Some of the children were found at casinos and truck stops, while others were advertised on the Internet. The operation was part of the Innocence Lost National Initiative, which was started in 2003 and has rescued nearly 900 children as of 2009. The initiative has also led to the conviction of 510 pimps, madams, and their associates and $3.1 million in seized assets, according to the FBI. FBI Director Robert Mueller said, "The sex trafficking of children remains one of the most violent and unforgivable crimes."

ON TARGET

During the Athens Olympics in 2004, the Greek government reported a 95 percent increase in the number of human trafficking victims. For the 2012 London Olympics, the United Kingdom's Metropolitan Police secured $949,000 to pay for a special unit to tackle the expected surge in people trafficking to supply the sex trade around the Olympic Village in London as construction workers and visitors pour into the area.

TRAFFICKING CHILDREN

Current estimates suggest that over one million children from around the world are trafficked each year. They may be exploited as cheap labor, forced to work in the sex trade, or kidnapped by rebel armies to fight as child soldiers. Very young children and babies may be sold for adoption.

Why Children?

Trafficking children is easy work for the traffickers, since the children are often too young to speak up for themselves. They are usually fit and healthy, with small, nimble fingers necessary for many types of work, yet they are less likely to put up a fight or escape from their captors. Sometimes, in poor countries, children are trafficked with the consent of their parents. Extreme poverty in some parts of the world can make parents so desperate to find ways to feed the rest of the family that they will accept cash payments for the sale of one or two of their children.

ON TARGET

The Asian tsunami in December 2004 killed tens of thousands of people and created many young orphans. In order to prevent traffickers from exploiting these extremely vulnerable children, the Indonesian government issued a ban on any children under 16 leaving the province of Aceh—one of the most hard-hit areas.

Girls or Boys?

Girls are often sold as child brides or exploited for sex work, while boys may be worth more in the illegal adoption trade. In China, a baby girl might be worth $1,028, but a boy might be worth up to $4,112 because boys have traditionally been valued more highly. Sometimes a child is trafficked as payment for a family debt.

◀ *This young girl is a domestic slave in Togo. She sells scissors and razor blades on the streets by day and does domestic chores for her owner by night. Togo has one of the highest rates of human trafficking of domestic slaves worldwide.*

◀ *This young Indian flower seller is typical of many trafficked children who are forced to work on the streets.*

Beggars

Children trafficked within Europe are often exploited as beggars; their handlers send them onto the streets of big cities, then collect their takings at the end of the day. A United Nations Children's Fund (UNICEF) report found that of the many Macedonian street children trafficked each year, 38 percent are lured by promises of a better life; 22 percent are lured by the prospect of money; 37 percent are promised work as maids or babysitters; 2 percent are sold by parents; and 1 percent are blackmailed.

▼ *These Chinese babies were rescued from an adoption trafficking gang working in China.*

BUSTED!

In 2009, Chinese police rescued 23 children in a nationwide crackdown on child trafficking from poor provinces. The children, ranging in age from young babies to eight years old, were frequently transported thousands of miles on trains or buses to new adoptive parents or organized begging gangs. Crowded public transport made detection difficult, but women traveling with a small child and lots of milk powder, yet little clothing or other possessions, were most likely to raise suspicion, according to the Chinese police.

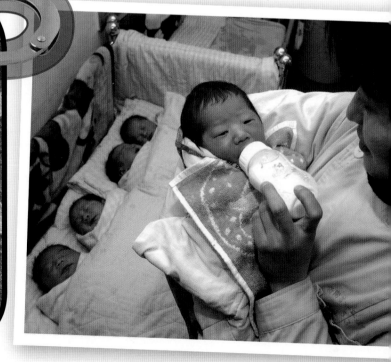

SOURCE COUNTRIES

The home country of a trafficked person is known as the source country. Source countries are found on every continent, including Europe, Australia, and the Americas, but typically a source country is a less economically developed country, or an area with a shifting, homeless, or marginalized population, such as a war zone.

Forced to Fight

Abducting children and forcing them to fight as child soldiers is a particularly brutal form of human trafficking that takes place within a source country's own borders. Children are often used by rebel armies and guerrilla groups because they are easy to kidnap and terrify into submission.

Because their abduction takes place in areas already disrupted by war, the problem is difficult to police, but organizations such as UNICEF and Caritas work hard to rehabilitate child soldiers when a conflict ends.

ON TARGET

In some parts of the world, labor exploitation is seen as a fact of life, and if victims don't actually leave the source country, then the crime is simply ignored. One of the main aims of the United Nations Office on Drugs and Crime (UNODC) is to educate governments about people trafficking and encourage them to introduce new laws to ensure that all traffickers are pursued and prosecuted.

◀ This photo was taken in 2000 and shows two boys who were enlisted in the Sierra Leonean army to fight against rebel forces.

◀ This Moldovan woman lives in hiding after escaping from Russia where she was trafficked into the sex industry. Moldova is one of the poorest countries in Europe and is a source country for people trafficking into the sex industry in particular.

Is Poverty the Problem?

Most victims of trafficking are poor and desperate. They are "soft targets" for the traffickers to recruit. Less poverty would undoubtedly reduce the supply of victims willing to be smuggled abroad. But does this mean that poverty in the source country is the cause of people trafficking? Some campaigners argue that those who create the demand for cheap labor, for prostitutes, for child soldiers, or for domestic slaves are to blame. Prevention also means tackling the corrupt officials who issue false passports, the airline staff who take bribes to turn a blind eye, or the customers who seek illegal adoptions, slave labor, or child brides.

▶ Many victims of people trafficking come from the less economically developed regions of Asia, Eastern Europe, and South America.

SOURCE COUNTRIES FOR HUMAN TRAFFICKING VICTIMS

NUMBERS OF REPORTED TRAFFICKING VICTIMS

- Very high
- High
- Medium
- Low
- Very low
- Not reported

IN TRANSIT

Recent estimates suggest that around 800,000 people are trafficked out of source countries and across international borders each year. Sometimes the victims are moved to a neighboring country. Sometimes they are moved through a number of countries and cover thousands of miles in a journey that may take up to a year to complete.

A Dangerous Journey

Many victims are not aware that they are being trafficked when they agree to leave their home countries. Some people cannot obtain travel documents, either legitimate or forged, so they allow themselves to be smuggled across borders in the hope that when they arrive at their destination, a better life awaits them. They are squeezed onto tiny, unsafe boats or cram themselves into airless container trucks. Some may even attempt to swim across dangerous stretches of water. Not everyone survives.

The Trail Goes Cold

Trafficking gangs sometimes use complex patterns through transit countries to avoid detection. A transit country may be chosen by traffickers because of its geographical location. Italy and Spain, with their southern borders facing Africa across the Mediterranean, are convenient transit countries for people arriving by boat from Africa.

ON TARGET

Interpol, the international police organization, aims to develop across-border cooperation between the police departments of its 188 member nations. In 2009, it coordinated a collaborative anti-trafficking training project between Italy (a transit and destination country) and Nigeria (a source country). "By hosting Nigerian police colleagues on Italian soil and by ensuring that they will be trained side by side . . . we will improve our joint ability to dismantle human trafficking rings," said Antonio Manganelli, Italy's Director of National Police. Nigeria has recently moved from the U.S. State Department's "watch list" (see page 9) to its top tier of countries that fully comply with its anti-trafficking standards.

◀ Some ports use X-ray machines to check container trucks for smuggled or trafficked people. This image clearly shows the people hidden in the truck.

▲ Although airports use many layers of security to prevent people entering countries illegally, people traffickers still manage to smuggle people through by swapping boarding passes or using forged papers.

Hub airports like Heathrow, in the United Kingdom, are popular because of their size and sheer volume of traffic. Other transit countries are chosen because of their weak immigration controls or their widespread corruption. Traffickers also rely on the fact that countries are often unwilling or unable to cooperate in international law enforcement arrangements.

Low Conviction Rates

A survey of 155 countries by the UNODC found that the number of countries with some form of anti-trafficking legislation increased from 33 percent in 2003 to 80 percent in 2008. However, the conviction rate in these countries remained disproportionately low. Two out of five countries have yet to convict a single trafficker. There are many reasons for this, but traffickers are quick to take advantage of the lack of across-border cooperation between different countries.

BUSTED!

One of the longest routes used by traffickers was revealed when six Chinese children were discovered in the United Kingdom. The children traveled over 17,400 miles (28,000 km) from China, via Brazil, to the United Kingdom, en route to a life of exploitation in illegal drug factories.

BORDER CONTROLS

A destination country is where trafficking victims are taken in order to exploit them. Some countries are both source and destination countries, though wealthier regions like the United States, Japan, and Western Europe are, on the whole, more likely to "import" victims than "export" them. In these regions, strict border controls are seen as essential in the fight against traffickers.

High-Tech Scrutiny

Strategies to combat people trafficking across international borders are increasingly high-tech. They include the introduction of biometric passports to make forgeries more difficult. Airport personnel use CCTV to spot fraudulent behavior including the swapping of boarding passes. The United States also uses technology such as unmanned planes and electronic sensors to identify smugglers and traffickers along its borders with Mexico and Canada. However, such strategies are expensive. Many countries continue to maintain huge border fences and wide ditches to make it difficult to cross borders illegally.

▼ *U.S. Border Control guards check the border fence that divides Mexico from the United States.*

ON TARGET

In the United States, the President's Interagency Task Force (PITF) coordinates the efforts of multiple government agencies to fight trafficking. Members include the Departments of State, Justice, Labor, Homeland Security, Health and Human Services, and Defense, among others. To oversee border controls, the Customs and Border Protection screens potential victims, and the Coast Guard works at sea to spot traffickers.

Who's the Target?

The emphasis placed by many countries on tighter border controls can sometimes work against the needs of the victims of people trafficking. Governments are under pressure to reduce the number of illegal immigrants, and many procedures are designed to screen out unwanted arrivals rather than identify vulnerable victims. At the point of entry, many victims don't yet know that they are being trafficked. If they are caught, they may be arrested as illegal immigrants while the traffickers remain unidentified. The United Nation's Special Rapporteur on Trafficking in Persons, Joy Ngozi Ezeilo, wants to see trafficking victims treated differently from illegal immigrants.

Regional Cooperation

One of the most effective ways for countries to combat people trafficking is to focus on across-border police operations with neighboring countries. Although there are still considerable differences in laws and police procedures between the countries of the Pacific region, progress is being made. For example, a conference in 2002 initiated the Bali Process whereby many Pacific countries aim to coordinate their anti-trafficking laws and policies for the extradition of offenders.

BUSTED!

In 2009, a Mexican national named Miguel Rugerio was convicted of trafficking young women from Mexico to the United States for the purpose of prostitution. Afterward, the Federal Bureau of Investigation (FBI) agent in charge of the investigation in Atlanta, Georgia said, "As a direct result of this investigation and recently passed human trafficking legislation in Mexico, Mexican law enforcement has, for the first time, been able to launch an investigation in an effort to combat this crime problem. We would like to express our gratitude to the Mexican consulate in Atlanta for their assistance in general and in assisting the victims that were being exploited by Mr. Rugerio."

▼ French police intercept a boat full of illegal immigrants heading for the Indian Ocean island of Mayotte. Coastguards and navies worldwide are constantly on the lookout for the illegal movement of people across the ocean, whether they be illegal immigrants or victims of people traffickers.

CASE STUDY: THE EUROPEAN UNION

The group of countries that make up the European Union (EU) has grown to 27 nations in recent years. The response to the issue of people trafficking has never been greater, with stronger police and intelligence sharing, new legislation, and greater recognition of the needs of victims. Yet the volume of people trafficking within Europe continues to grow.

Rapid Expansion

Until the last decade, the EU's membership was limited to the wealthier countries of Western Europe—countries like Germany, France, Italy, and the United Kingdom. But after the collapse of the old Soviet Union from 1989 onward, many of the less economically developed countries of Eastern Europe joined the EU. The EU underwent a major expansion in 2004 and again in 2007, incorporating countries like Slovenia, Lithuania, Romania, and Bulgaria.

THE EUROPEAN UNION

■ Current members

■ Hoping to join

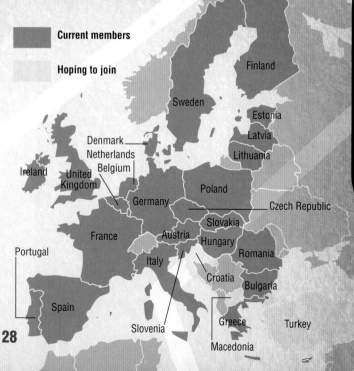

Finland
Sweden
Estonia
Latvia
Denmark
Netherlands
Lithuania
Ireland
Belgium
United Kingdom
Poland
Germany
Czech Republic
Slovakia
Slovenia
Austria
Hungary
France
Romania
Portugal
Italy
Croatia
Bulgaria
Spain
Slovenia
Greece
Turkey
Macedonia

ON TARGET

Information sharing and international cooperation are key tools in the fight against people trafficking in the EU. National police departments can now share details about criminals through the European law enforcement agency Europol, while the European Arrest Warrant allows for the arrest and transfer of suspects between EU states without the need for lengthy extradition procedures.

BUSTED!

In 2008, officers from the UK's Serious Organised Crime Agency (SOCA) took an Albanian man already convicted of trafficking crimes to Lithuania to give evidence against two individuals responsible for supplying women to traffickers. This joint operation with the Lithuanian police resulted in six other trafficking groups being identified in the United Kingdom.

◄ *The map shows the current members of the European Union in blue and the countries that are negotiating to join the EU in yellow.*

The Schengen Agreement

One of the guiding principles of the EU is the free movement of goods and people across its internal borders. Member nations who have signed an agreement known as the Schengen Agreement do not maintain border controls with neighboring member countries, though not every member country has signed this agreement (the United Kingdom, for example, still maintains its border controls). This allows travel across the EU, from Slovakia in the east to France in the west, without a passport. Criminals have been quick to take advantage of this, trafficking vulnerable people from the poor areas of Eastern Europe into wealthier destination countries, such as Germany, with ease.

▲ *Cars pass through a border control point on the border between Slovakia and Ukraine, which has now become one of the eastern borders of the European Union. Once in Slovakia, people may travel passport-free all the way to France.*

▶ *Rob Wainwright, Director of Europol, says, "This is a time of great opportunity for Europe and police cooperation in the EU."*

A New External Border

Of course, the EU's external borders maintain the usual border controls, and it is illegal to enter the EU without appropriate documents. But several major source and transit countries for people trafficking, such as Turkey and Ukraine, are now only one external border crossing away. The EU border with Ukraine alone covers almost 1,800 miles (2,900 km) from Poland in the north to Bulgaria in the south, and Ukrainian anti-trafficking police estimate that only 20 percent of people who attempt to cross it illegally are being caught.

CAUGHT IN THE ACT

Catching and prosecuting people traffickers isn't easy. Some countries, including many African countries, have open or "porous" borders across which traffickers and their victims can move without challenge. But porous borders aren't the only problem. Destination countries also need to ensure that they have strong laws and enough properly trained police to enforce them.

Success in Ghana

Many Ghanaians, especially women and children, have become victims of trafficking to countries in the West Africa sub-region as well as Europe, Asia, and the Americas. In 2005, Ghana passed a law against people trafficking, but this law was not tested until 2006 when Deputy Police Superintendent Patience Quaye pursued and prosecuted a man who had sold his nine-year-old stepson to strangers in Nigeria. The offender was extradited and sentenced to six years in prison—the first successful prosecution for the crime of people trafficking in Ghana.

Quaye, who received training from the UNODC, later led an operation that convicted a group of traffickers bringing Chinese women into the country (see page 19) and was recognized by President Obama as an anti-trafficking "hero."

BUSTED!

Police departments are increasingly using officers trained in undercover work to catch people traffickers as they attempt to sell or exploit their victims. Four Bulgarian traffickers were arrested in northern Greece in 2009 for trying to sell a Bulgarian woman for $2,750 to undercover police officers posing as nightclub owners.

▼ A university student in Benin City, Nigeria, walks past a poster encouraging women to fight against prostitution and people trafficking.

Proactive Policing

The police rely heavily on the evidence of victims when prosecuting traffickers. However, proactive policing, where police use other investigative techniques to gather evidence, is often more likely to lead to a conviction. These techniques might include tapping the phones of suspects, covert surveillance of suspects, undercover work, and a close scrutiny of commercial activity, such as banking transactions, property rental, and the use of advertising to recruit potential victims.

Prosecuting the "Customer"

Another way for destination countries to combat trafficking is to interrupt the demand for slave labor or sex workers. In the United States in 2009, the Human Trafficking Rescue Project in Kansas City conducted an undercover operation in which task force officers placed ads asking for underage prostitutes on the Internet. Under U.S. law, anyone who attempts to obtain underage children for sex is considered a trafficker, and those who responded to the ads were arrested and charged.

▲ After months of undercover work, police raided a suburban house in Belfast, Northern Ireland, in order to free victims of people trafficking. Three women were rescued during the raid.

ON TARGET

The United States Trafficking Victims Protection Act (TVPA) of 2000 is the act that created the President's Interagency Task Force (PITF) in order to coordinate government-wide efforts to combat people trafficking.

► Some people think it is not fair to prosecute men who pay for sex with trafficked women, as they may be unaware that the women have been trafficked.

LOOPHOLES IN THE LAW

Despite new laws to stop traffickers and protect their victims, many loopholes remain. Laws protecting employees, for example, often exclude migrant or temporary workers. Traffickers sometimes persuade their victims to claim asylum in order to get them into a destination country. Meanwhile, genuine asylum seekers and refugees may become vulnerable to traffickers while they wait to hear whether they will be allowed to stay.

A Revolving Door of Abuse

In 2007, the Malaysian government passed an Anti-Trafficking in Persons Act in an attempt to tackle widescale people trafficking across its borders with Indonesia, Thailand, and Burma. However, the Malaysian government also continues to confiscate the passports of migrant workers from Indonesia, making them vulnerable to people traffickers and open to exploitation by their Malaysian employers. In addition, human rights organizations have reported cases where Malaysian officials simply dump Burmese refugees on the Thai border, often directly into the hands of people traffickers. Many victims are then trafficked straight back into Malaysia. Local activists have called such treatment "a revolving door of abuse."

ON TARGET

The state of New Jersey has recently closed a legal loophole by introducing a new law to protect foreign-born women from exploitation by unscrupulous employment agencies. Anyone operating an international marriage agency or a service that brings women to the United States to work as nannies or maids is now required to undergo a criminal background check to see if they have any previous convictions for offenses such as people trafficking.

▼ *Illegal immigrants in a detention center in Malaysia in 2009.*

BUSTED!

In 2009, French police dismantled a camp of illegal immigrants close to Calais, known locally as "The Jungle," detaining 278 people including 132 children. The French government hailed the raid as a victory in the fight against people traffickers who preyed on vulnerable victims living in the camp. Aid workers disagreed, saying that the only people penalized by the raid were the illegal immigrants themselves.

► *French police arrive to start dismantling the illegal immigrants' camp known as "The Jungle" close to Calais, France.*

The Issue of Asylum

Asylum seekers are people who enter a foreign country and ask for a "safe haven" from persecution in their home country. In recent years, the procedures for admitting asylum seekers to a number of countries have been tightened because of fears of terrorism and concerns about illegal immigrants who seek to abuse the system. But deciding whether someone is a genuine asylum seeker, an illegal immigrant, or a victim of trafficking isn't easy, and the traffickers are often quick to exploit this uncertainty.

Children in the United Kingdom

A recent report has highlighted the case of Chinese children trafficked into the United Kingdom to work in marijuana factories around the country. Typically, a trafficker tells the children to destroy their travel documents on the plane before they arrive. They then enter the United Kingdom and are picked up by immigration officials, who cannot send them home because they say they are under 18. The children are placed in temporary care homes by social services, and then they contact their "handlers" via a pre-programmed cell phone and run away. Social workers are powerless to stop them without a court order, though they do what they can to confiscate phones and investigate telephone calls.

POLICE AND WELFARE

Those seeking to end people trafficking in all its forms still face many obstacles. Nevertheless, the police and other agencies are making significant progress in one key area: victim support. This may include access to healthcare, clothing and shelter, witness protection programs, and visas that give victims legitimate legal status.

Breaking the Cycle

If victims of trafficking are treated as illegal immigrants or as criminals, it is likely that they will be deported to their country of origin. Yet often, this simply increases their vulnerability, and they may end up being trafficked again. However, if victims are allowed access to safe, secure housing, to counselors who listen to their stories, and to lawyers who offer free legal services, they are more likely to break the cycle of desperation. Some victims are even beginning to pursue compensation from their traffickers in the courts.

ON TARGET

Europe's first dedicated center for victims of people trafficking opened in Sheffield in the United Kingdom in 2006. The Human Trafficking Centre is run by the Association of Chief Police Officers and brings together academics, police, lawyers, and immigration officials under one roof to help victims with issues such as housing. It also works closely with the government-funded Poppy Project, which offers accommodation and support to women who are victims of sex trafficking.

▼ *This Lithuanian girl was rescued from traffickers and given shelter by the Poppy Project, a UK government-funded organization.*

Sending a Signal

When the police protect victims (rather than punish them), a clear signal goes out to other victims—they have nothing to fear by coming forward. Welfare initiatives by the police also send a clear signal to the traffickers themselves—they cannot rely on the victims' fear of being caught. Protecting the identity of witnesses—usually the victims themselves—is a key aspect of police welfare. In practice, this is difficult because most traffickers already know the identity of any witnesses, so safe houses and, in some cases, new identities are necessary to ensure a witness's safety.

Reuniting Families

In China, where around 40,000 children are reported missing each year, the task of reuniting trafficked children with their families is a daunting one. However, a government database collects DNA from family members, and this is compared with that of children rescued by the police. In 2009, Chinese police also launched a website displaying pictures of trafficked children in the hope that parents will recognize them. Tang Weihua, a mother whose son was abducted in 1999, says, "The site is a blessing for desperate parents like us who have nearly lost hope."

BUSTED!

A charity in Bosnia-Herzegovina has found that those victims who are given support such as free legal aid are more likely to testify against their traffickers in court. However, human rights organizations argue that the granting of visas and accommodation to victims should not be dependent on their willingness to cooperate with the police.

▶ A Chinese man hugs his son, one of 60 children rescued from people traffickers operating in southwest China in 2009.

WORKING WITH NGOs

While governments grapple with new laws as part of a long-term strategy to combat people trafficking, some valuable work is being done at a more local level. Many non-governmental organizations (NGOs) and community groups are able to focus on specific grassroots issues. They provide a vital "bridge" between victims and the police.

Building Trust

Some NGOs offer safe houses for victims of trafficking, where they can find shelter, receive counseling, and develop new skills. The Coalition to Abolish Slavery and Trafficking (CAST) provides comprehensive services for victims in Los Angeles, California, including food, shelter, health services, education, job training, and language skills. Since 2005, it has been a partner in the Human Trafficking Task Force, along with the Los Angeles Police Department and other NGOs, in order to improve tactics for identifying, rescuing, and assisting victims, as well as prosecuting the traffickers.

ON TARGET

Local employers in the Philippines have joined the fight against traffickers by participating in the Corporate Apprenticeship program—a joint initiative between the UNODC and the Philippine Department for Social Welfare and Development. Trafficking victims are accepted as apprentices for periods of six months to a year to gain on-the-job training in factory work, hospitality, and other businesses, so that they can build up the skills that make them less vulnerable to further exploitation.

◀ Esohe Aghatise, the director of Associazione Iroko Onlus in Turin, Italy, gives free advice to a rescued victim of people trafficking. The organization provides counseling, legal and emotional support, food, and basic job training for trafficked Nigerians.

▶ Moldovan police arrest a "trafficker" at the end of a two-week training course on anti-trafficking for police in Moldova.

Training in Moldova

Victims are often wary of giving evidence to the police out of fear of recrimination from the traffickers. When police in Moldova took part in a two-week field exercise, they were challenged to develop a criminal case that could be successfully prosecuted in court without relying on the victim's testimony. After training, the police began to refer victims directly to local NGOs providing welfare services and protection. Some victims, in return, felt more able to trust the police.

Community Action in Indonesia

In one district of Indonesia, people were very concerned about the high number of girls being trafficked out of the community, but little was being done to combat the crime. So a local task force was set up, and by 2008 dozens of local organizations were working alongside police and community leaders to help vulnerable families start businesses, inform farmers about trafficking, and assist in law enforcement. Their efforts succeeded in driving traffickers away from their villages and protected hundreds of girls from trafficking for sexual exploitation. Other districts in the region are now following their example.

BUSTED!

In Burkina Faso, West Africa, local truckers have joined forces with transportation workers' unions and community groups to intercept victims of people trafficking. By establishing an anti-trafficking alert system at bus stations and other transportation pick-up points, they have rescued hundreds of child victims, according to a U.S. government report.

◀ Most of these Indian children were either bonded laborers or were forced to work all day on weaving looms, making carpets or saris. They were rescued by an Indian NGO and now attend a school in India where they receive an education and are given help to recover from their ordeal.

RAISING AWARENESS

There are many reasons behind the growth in people trafficking. Greed, corruption, poverty, and indifference all play a part. Lack of awareness is also a factor. Victims don't understand the dangers they face when they accept a job from a "friend" abroad. The police may not understand that many victims are too afraid to speak out. In addition, the victim may not have the language skills to explain his or her position. Raising awareness about these issues through training and public information is a key tool in the fight against people trafficking.

Empowering Women

Attitudes need to change, as well as laws. For example, many women fall victim to sex traffickers because of sexist attitudes that perpetuate a view that women's bodies are mere commodities. These same women are then afraid to report what has happened to them because of the shame attached to prostitution. Enabling women to achieve financial independence and find a voice within their communities is a significant goal for many anti-trafficking agencies.

▼ *A huge poster warns of the dangers of people trafficking in Moldova. It reads, "You are not a commodity."*

ON TARGET

Major George Vanikiotis is one of Greece's most knowledgeable anti-trafficking experts. He directs operations for the Anti-Trafficking Unit and provides training to police officers, prosecutors, health professionals, labor inspectors, and NGOs throughout the country. He also leads anti-trafficking seminars at high schools and universities and has recently been recognized by the U.S. State Department as one of its "heroes acting to end modern-day slavery."

BUSTED!

In 2006, a South African soccer team, the Kaizer Chiefs, wore T-shirts with the message "Blow the Whistle" and a telephone number to report trafficking activity during a televised pre-game warm-up. This event inaugurated the country's national Human Trafficking Awareness campaign in the lead up to the 2010 World Cup.

Responding to Emergencies

The UNODC also runs campaigns with NGOs, distributing written information and contacting actual and potential victims of trafficking. For example, when war broke out in Lebanon in 2006, thousands of domestic workers from Sri Lanka, Ethiopia, and the Philippines were left behind when their employers were evacuated. Having lost their jobs and official resident status, these workers quickly became vulnerable to traffickers operating in the region. The UNODC responded by putting out emergency information in various languages and setting up a telephone hotline.

Educating Vulnerable Communities

The UNODC helps to make people aware of the risks from traffickers by making public service announcements, which are broadcast on radio and TV stations in numerous languages throughout the world. In Colombia, in South America, UNODC helped to produce a prime time television soap opera about human trafficking. Broadcast nightly to millions of viewers, the series exposed common traffickers' tricks, such as using the Internet to advertise non-existent jobs, and explained where victims could seek help.

▶ *Oscar-winning actress Mira Sorvino was appointed as a UN Goodwill Ambassador on human trafficking by Antonio Maria Costa, Executive Director of the UNODC. The UN uses Goodwill Ambassadors, who are all celebrities such as movie stars or athletes, to attract attention to their work.*

TAKING A STAND

Everyone can get involved in the fight against people trafficking. We can talk about the issues and help raise awareness in our communities. We can also make good choices about the services we use and the products we buy in order to avoid supporting the exploitation of other people.

Public Campaigns

People trafficking takes place in almost every country around the world. Yet the general public is often unaware of its reach. Public campaigns play an important role in highlighting the issues so that people can begin to ask questions, demand better laws, and expect more successful prosecutions. "There is a lot of ignorance about modern slavery. There is also a lot of good will to fight it," said Antonio Maria Costa, of the UNODC, at the launch of the UN's Blue Heart campaign in 2009.

Fair Trade

Where have those blueberries come from? What about that cheap T-shirt? And who sewed all those sequins onto that "bargain" party dress? Ordinary shoppers can play a part in preventing people trafficking by demanding that the goods they buy involve a fair wage for those who produced them. The Fairtrade mark on coffee, chocolate, or bananas is one indication that workers have been paid a fair wage for their labor. Organizations such as the Clean Clothes Campaign also help inform consumers about those companies that may be guilty of exploiting their workforce.

ON TARGET

The UN's Blue Heart campaign strives to raise awareness about human trafficking and its impact on society. It also wants to inspire people to get involved and stop this crime. The campaign uses the Blue Heart logo, which represents the sadness of trafficking victims and the coldheartedness of those who buy and sell other people.

◀ Delegates at a UN convention to discuss people trafficking. The blue heart is the symbol of the UN's people trafficking campaign.

▲ *Tomato pickers work in Florida. Thanks to the campaign led by the Coalition of Immokalee Workers (see Busted! box), they are now less open to exploitation.*

Consumer Power

Consumers can also check out the background and ethical standards of a wide range of companies by looking at one of the many "ethical shopping" sites online. They can then choose to avoid those shops and supermarkets whose overseas suppliers fail to demonstrate good labor practices. The clothing store Gap faced heavy public criticism when it was discovered that some of its clothing had been produced by children working in sweatshops in India. After the story broke, Gap decided to tighten up its checks on suppliers to make sure they complied with its ethical standards.

BUSTED!

Migrant tomato pickers in the state of Florida have at times been subject to highly exploitative practices by their employers. However, a group of workers formed the Coalition of Immokalee Workers and conducted a campaign which eventually succeeded in persuading Burger King, a major customer for Florida's tomato growers, to agree that forced labor practices would not be tolerated by the company.

GLOSSARY

abduction kidnapping

asylum seekers people who seek refuge in a foreign country because of threats or harm in their own country

biometric passports passports that store someone's unique physical data such as fingerprints

bonded labor/debt bondage where people are forced to work to pay off a debt to their employer; debts are often so inflated (or the "wage" is so low) that the workers are never able to pay off the debt and may pass it on to their child.

brothel a house where prostitutes work

Caritas an international Catholic organization that focuses on relieving poverty and helping in emergencies

corrupt open to bribes

covert surveillance secret cameras; undercover scrutiny

deportation official expulsion to another country

displaced homeless or living in temporary shelter because of war or natural disaster

DNA (deoxyribonucleic acid) long molecules inside living cells that contain genetic information

Europol the European Law Enforcement Organization

exploit treat someone unfairly for personal profit

extradition agreement between countries that they will hand over criminals to be tried in the country where they committed a crime

forced labor where people are forced against their will to work for an employer for very low wages

foreman someone who organizes the work, transport, pay, and accommodation for a group of workers

fraudulent obtained by deceit or forgery

guerrilla groups groups of unofficial soldiers or rebel fighters

heroin a very addictive drug made from morphine, a chemical found in opium

hub airport an international airport that travelers use to make connections

illegal immigrant someone who enters a country illegally and remains without permission

Interpol the International Criminal Police Organization

in transit on the way

laundering concealing illegal profits

legitimate legal

marginalized not accepted as part of a regular community or society

migrants people who travel around, usually in search of work

NGO (non-governmental organization) the collective name for legally established organizations that work for change or provide a useful service at a local, national, or international level

people smuggling moving people illegally across borders

pimp someone who makes money by controlling prostitutes

porous borders borders without adequate security, such as fences or ditches, to stop people from crossing illegally

prostitution offering sex for money

refugees people who have been forced to flee to another country to escape war or natural disaster

rehabilitate help someone back into normal society

soft targets people who are most vulnerable to people traffickers

source country the home country of victims of trafficking

transatlantic slave trade the shipment of people from Africa to the Americas for the purposes of slavery

UN (United Nations) an international organization founded after World War II with the aim of maintaining peace and security between nations

UN.GIFT United Nations Global Initiative to Fight Human Trafficking

UNICEF (United Nations Children's Fund) founded by the United Nations to address the needs of children and mothers in particular

UNODC United Nations Office on Drugs and Crime

visa a document that gives someone permission to enter a foreign country

FURTHER INFORMATION

Books

Hart, Joyce. *Human Trafficking (In the News)*, Rosen Publishing, 2009.

Lankford, Ronald Jr. (editor). *Slavery Today (At Issue. Social Issues)*, Greenhaven Press, 2010.

Stearman, Kaye. *Human Trafficking Around the World (Global Issues)*, Rosen Central, 2011.

Web Sites

www.state.gov/g/tip/rls/tiprpt/
Part of the U.S. Department of the State web site where you can access the annual Trafficking in Persons report for the current year, as well as an archive of past reports.

www.unodc.org/blueheart/
This is the site for the United Nations Blue Heart Campaign to raise awareness about people trafficking and its victims.

www.ciw-online.org/slavery.html
The link to the Coalition of Immokalee Workers' anti-slavery campaign, focusing on exploitation of agricultural workers.

www.amnestyusa.org/artists-for-amnesty/human-trafficking/page.do?id=1121006
This is Amnesty International's web site dedicated to ending human trafficking.

www.humantrafficking.org/
A resource with a wealth of knowledge on human trafficking taking place all over the world.

www.ungift.org/ungift/en/humantrafficking/stories.html
Click on this page to read survivors' stories from around the world.

www.unicef-irc.org/
UNICEF's web site dedicated to research efforts about child-related issues, including child trafficking.

Note to parents and teachers: Every effort has been made by the publishers to ensure that these web sites are suitable for children, that they are of the highest educational value, and that they contain no inappropriate or offensive material. However, because of the nature of the Internet, it is impossible to guarantee that the contents of these sites will not be altered. We strongly advise that Internet access is supervised by a responsible adult.

INDEX

SERIES CONTENTS

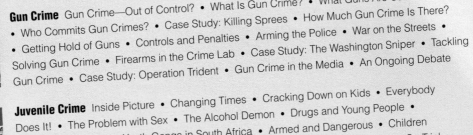